D1226527

Crows

Steven Otfinoski

Published in 2015 by Cavendish Square Publishing, LLC
243 5th Avenue, Suite 136, New York, NY 10016

First Edition

Website: cavendishsq.com

Library of Congress Cataloging-in-Publication Data

Otfinoski, Steven.
Crows / Steven Otfinoski.
pages cm. — (Backyard safari)
Includes index.
ISBN 978-1-62712-831-5 (hardcover) ISBN 978-1-62712-832-2 (paperback) ISBN 978-1-62712-833-9 (ebook)
1. Crows--Juvenile literature. I. Title.

QL696.P2367O74 2014
598.8'64--dc23

2013047682

Editorial Director: Dean Miller
Editor: Andrew Coddington
Copy Editor: Cynthia Roby
Art Director: Jeffrey Talbot
Designer: Joseph Macri
Photo Researcher: J8 Media
Production Manager: Jennifer Ryder-Talbot
Production Editor: David McNamara

The photographs in this book are used by permission and through the courtesy of: Cover photo by Roberta Olenick/All Canada Photos / Getty Images; EBFoto / Shutterstock.com, 4; LeoGrand / E+ / Getty Images, 5; age fotostock / SuperStock, 6; Justin Russ / Shutterstock.com, 8; Joe Klementovich / Joe Klementovich / Getty Images, 9; © birdpix / Alamy, 10; Bruce Obee / All Canada Photos / Getty Images, 13; Glenn Bartley / All Canada Photos / Getty Images, 15; Cultura Limited / SuperStock, 17; David Tipling / Lonely Planet Images / Getty Images, 18; Tim Zurowski / All Canada Photos / Getty Images, 20; Bruce Obee / All Canada Photos /Getty Images, 20; Norbert Kurzka - Photography / Flickr / Getty Images, 21; Jared Hobbs / All Canada Photos / Getty Images, 21; Bartomeu Borrell /age fotostock / Getty Images, 21; JIM ZIPP / Photo Researchers / Getty Images, 21; William Leaman / Alamy, 23; perlphoto/Shutterstock.com, 24; John Block / The Image Bank / Getty Images, 27.

Printed in the United States of America

Contents

Introduction

Have you ever watched baby spiders hatch from a silky egg sac, or seen a butterfly sip nectar from a flower? If you have, you know how wonderful it is to discover nature for yourself. Each book in the Backyard Safari series takes you step-by-step on an easy outdoor adventure, and then helps you identify the animals you've found. You'll also learn ways to attract, observe, and protect these valuable creatures. As you read, be on the lookout for the Safari Tips and Trek Talk facts sprinkled throughout the book. Ready? The fun starts just steps from your back door!

ONE

Crow World

Have you ever walked or ridden past a cornfield and noticed a flock of crows in it? If you disturbed these birds, you would have seen them scatter into the sky, darkening it with their black bodies, making loud "Caw! Caw!" sounds.

A large group of crows in flight is an impressive sight.

Crows are among the most common birds in North America. But they are uncommon in many ways. Crows are fearless, clever, and among the most intelligent of all animals. These amazing birds can identify and memorize a human face in a crowd of people and recognize it again for up to two years. Crows in **captivity** can be taught to solve puzzles, recognize symbols, count objects, and even imitate sounds and words—much like a parrot.

Hungry Scavengers

Crows have a healthy appetite and must eat eleven ounces (312 grams) of food each day to remain healthy. Crows on an average farm will eat 670 pounds (304 kilograms) of insects in one growing season. They will eat almost anything. Farmers consider them pests because they eat their corn and other grains and seeds. But crows are also farmers' friends, because they eat many insects and rodents, such as mice, that are harmful to crops. Crows also eat fruits, earthworms, the eggs of other birds and their young, snakes, frogs, **carrion**, and anything edible in your garbage can! Crows will even eat shellfish, such as clams and oysters. They fly into the sky and drop the shells on rocks to break them open

Crows will eat almost anything. This one is getting his meal from a bag of garbage.

so they can eat the animal's soft body inside. They will drop nuts on roads and then wait for cars to run over them and break the shells so then they can eat the meat inside.

Even more amazing, some crows can make and use tools to retrieve food. The only other animals capable of doing this are elephants and chimpanzees. Scientists studied the New Caledonia crow, which is capable of making and using tools. It lives on the island of New Caledonia in the Pacific Ocean. The scientists attached tiny video cameras to the tails of these crows to record their movements. What they witnessed was incredible. The New Caledonia crows would break twigs off the branches of trees, and smooth and bend them. They would then push the sticks into the soft surface of rotting trees to uncover **grubs** to eat. Other times, they would take dry grass stems and poke them into the nests of other birds to find eggs or hatchlings, which are newborn birds, to eat. If a tool was particularly useful, the crow would save it to use another time.

Roosting and Mobbing

Crows are extremely social birds and live in small family groups that number from four to seven birds. But during the fall and winter months, they will fly as far as fifty miles (eighty kilometers) to join up with

These crows are roosting for the night in tree branches.

hundreds or thousands of other crows to find a common place to **roost**. They start their journey in the afternoon and make rest stops along the way, picking up more and more crows at each stop. By nightfall, they arrive at their roosting place, usually a distant spot protected by trees. After a good night's sleep, they will fly away the next morning, returning to their feeding grounds. Scientists are not certain why crows roost this way. It may be to protect themselves from **predators** such as hawks, horned owls, and raccoons. Or it could be that they gather at a place where there is plenty of food.

When one of these predators comes around, the crows carry out another defense called **mobbing**. A flock of crows will harass and annoy the predator until it grows uneasy and flies or runs away. They will fly about or even dive-bomb the other bird or animal, squawk nosily, or even **defecate** on it. They will continue this behavior for up to ten minutes, if it takes that long to get rid of the intruder. Why crows mob is somewhat of a mystery. Some scientists believe that the predator the

Trek Talk
Crows and other blackbirds—several **species** of birds in which both male and female are largely, if not entirely, black—aren't the only birds that mob predators. Jays, chickadees, terns, and mockingbirds have all been observed mobbing.

crows harass is not interested in bothering such a large flock of birds. They think crows may mob to teach their fledglings, or young, to identify their enemies.

Crows in Trouble

Human beings are among crows' greatest enemies. Farmers shoot them to keep them from eating their crops. Hunters shoot them for sport. Crow hunting is allowed in every state but Hawaii, and there is no limit to how many a hunter can kill during hunting season. Organizations such as the Crows.net Project are trying to put an end to crow hunting in the United States. Its organizers believe that the killing of these highly intelligent birds is wrong.

A hunter is looking for crows to shoot.

Crows have more to fear than predators and

humans. They are vulnerable to diseases, especially West Nile **virus**, which is spread by mosquitos. Since 1999, West Nile has killed 45 percent of American crows. Loss of **habitat**, on the other hand, is not a problem for crows. They are among the most adaptable of birds and will thrive in towns and cities where they live off food in dumpsters and garbage cans.

Raising Young

Crows are good parents. Unlike many birds, they usually stay with one mate for life. After mating, both the father and mother help build a nest high in a treetop or along a hedge. The female lays four to six pale blue-green eggs. After eighteen days of incubation, or the mother sitting on the eggs, the young hatch. They will remain in the nest for up to thirty-five days, while the male and female feed them insects and seeds. After six to eight weeks, they are independent and may set out on their own. However, many young crows will stay with their parents for up to five years.

A mother crow feeds her hungry nestlings mouth-to-mouth.

Many crows do not survive the first year of life. They die

either in the egg or as nestlings, that is, when they are too young to fly. If they can survive the first year, they can live as long as seventeen to twenty-one years.

A Crow's Body

The common crow has a body that measures eighteen to nineteen inches (forty-six to forty-eight centimeters) in length. Its wings and body **plumage**, or overall feathers, are a glossy black. When a crow **molts**, its old feathers turn brownish in color and appear scaly. Its new feathers are sleek and black. The crow has a wingspan of three feet (one meter), and a short tail that is either roundish or squared at the end. Its black beak is thin, yet strong and pointy. A crow's eyes are dark brown in color, although the nestling's eyes are blue. They

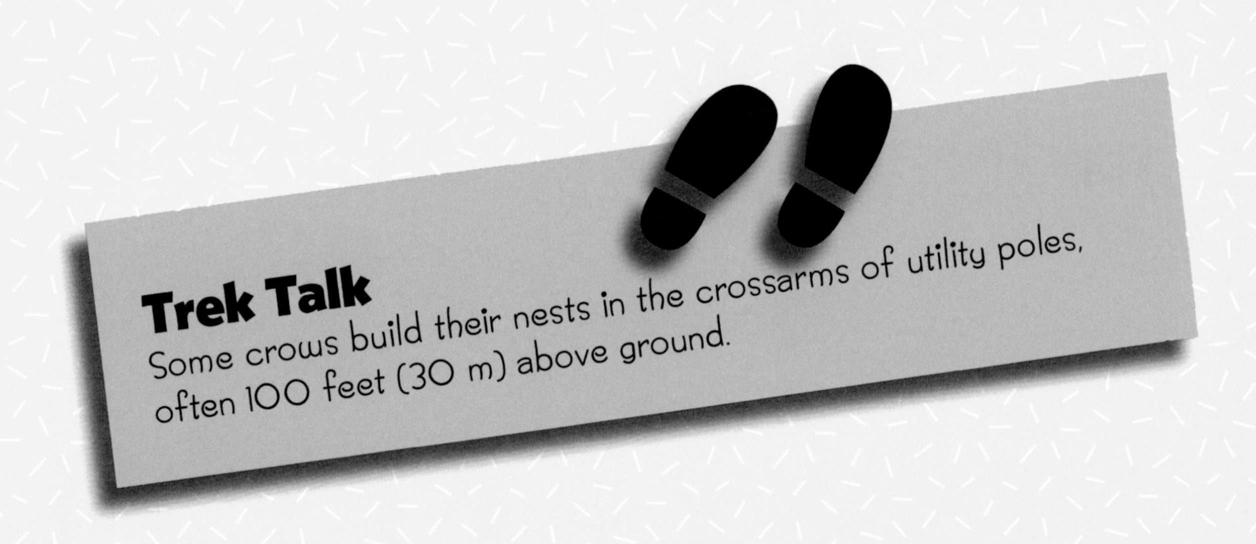

have better eyesight than most other birds and animals. They are able to see many colors and can accurately spot very small insects, animals, and other items from long distances. Crows have sturdy feet, as they spend much of their time on the ground. The bird's four thick toes are about the same length. The total length of a crow's footprint is approximately three inches (8 cm).

Crows belong to a family of blackbirds that includes close to forty species. Among their relatives are ravens, magpies, rooks, jays, and jackdaws. They are found everywhere in the world but Antarctica. Are you ready to go looking for these fascinating birds? It's time to go on safari.

Trek Talk

A group of crows is called a "murder." This unusual name may have come from the old superstition that these all-black birds are an **omen** of death.

TWO

You Are the Explorer

Crows are sturdy, highly intelligent birds.

You can find crows on safari in your backyard almost any time of year. In very cold parts of the country, they may migrate to warmer, southern areas in the winter, but they reside in most parts of the country year-round.

What Do I Wear?

- Light, casual, and comfortable clothes in spring and summer
- Heavier, warmer clothes in fall and winter
- If sunny and hot, a hat with a brim
- Sunglasses
- Sunscreen

What Do I Take?

- A pair of binoculars
- Digital camera
- Notebook
- Colored pens or pencils

Where Do I Go?

Crows will most likely be attracted to these plants, trees, or areas in your yard:

- Seed-producing plants such as sunflowers
- Vegetable gardens
- Flowering trees, including fruit trees

- Fence posts where they can perch
- Wooded areas
- Grassy areas

If your yard doesn't offer several of these features, here are a few other safari locations you can try:

- Meadows or fields
- Orchards
- Open woodlands
- Public parks
- Forests
- Town or city dumps
- Cemeteries

Always have an adult with you if you are going beyond your yard.

Safari Tip

Crows don't like noises. If you have wind chimes or bells in your backyard, remove them. If you have a dog or cat, you might want to keep them indoors when you go on safari so they don't scare off the crows.

What Do I Do?

- Use your binoculars to locate and get a close-up look at any crows. Crows are cautious around people. You'll have to be patient in viewing them.
- Snap a photo with your camera of any crows you see.
- Make a brief entry in your notebook of every crow sighting, answering questions such as these: Is the crow alone or part of a murder? If there is more than one crow, how do they relate to one another? What is it doing? Is it eating or perching? If it's eating, what is it eating—an animal, insect, plant, or garbage? What sounds does it make?
- Using your digital picture as a reference, sketch a drawing of a crow and color it in.
- Spend about a half hour to one hour on safari.
- Clean up the area and take everything with you when you leave.

A boy makes friends with a hungry crow.

How many crows did you see during your safari? If the answer is none, don't worry. Every safari is different. You are sure to have more success on your next adventure. Plan to go on safari again soon.

If you were lucky enough to take pictures of a crow, transfer your photos onto the computer and print them when you get home. Share your notebook with a friend or your family. Take someone on safari with you next time. Now it's time to learn more about your backyard visitors!

THREE

A Guide to Crows

Since the crow is part of the blackbird family and all these birds are completely or mostly black, identifying the individual species can be a challenge. Most of the blackbirds pictured in this chapter, such as the common crow, can be found in many parts of the United States. By looking at the photographs and reading their unique characteristics, you should be able to distinguish between them while you are on safari.

Ask yourself these questions. The answers will help you use the guide to identify the crows and their close relatives that you see in your backyard.

- What colors other than black does the bird have on its body, and where?
- How large is its body? Its tail?
- What sounds does it make?
- How does it behave around other birds?
- What kinds of food does it seem to like?

Trek Talk

Magpies are known as the "thieves of the bird world." They are attracted to small, bright shiny objects, such as jewelry. They will steal these little treasures and carry them off to their nests.

By matching the colors, size, sounds, and other characteristics with the photos in the crow guide, you should be able to identify other blackbirds you see on safari. Here is a sample entry:

COMMON CROW

Color(s): Green (back), black (chin), line of violet below chin

Size: Medium

Location: Perched on branch of tree

Activity: Cawing and flapping its wings

Crow Guide

Fish Crow

Northwestern Crow

Common Raven

Chihuahuan Raven

Black-billed Magpie

Yellow-billed Magpie

FOUR

Try This! Projects You Can Do

Here are four projects you can do to attract crows to your backyard and report on what you see.

Create a Crow Corner in Your Backyard

Like all birds, crows like to eat. You can attract them to your backyard and watch their fascinating behavior by creating a crow corner with food and water. You don't have to add all these things to your crow corner, but the more you do, the more likely you will draw crows to it.

What Do I Need?

- One or more of the following: sunflower seeds, peanuts in the shell, cracked corn, cat or dog food (dry kibble)
- Wooden poles
- A birdbath (store bought)

- A water hose or watering can
- A shovel

What Do I Do?

- Pick a designated area in your backyard for your crow corner, preferably near a window so you can easily observe the crows that stop by.
- Scatter your choice of crow food on the ground. Crows prefer to eat their food there and not from a bird feeder.
- Plant the poles in the ground. If the ground is hard, first dig a hole with a shovel.

Place a wooden board across the poles for the crows to use as a perch. Crows will also roost on fences and gates.

- Place the birdbath in the center of your crow corner and fill it with water. Crows love water and will enjoy drinking and bathing in your birdbath.
- Remove the items from your yard that make loud noises, such as wind chimes and bells. Crows don't like loud noises.

A crow caws to his fellow crows. What is he telling them?

Be patient. Crows are cautious when it comes to feeding areas. You'll probably get other birds, such as blue jays, coming to eat the food you put out before the crows arrive. Once the crows find your crow corner, however, they will return regularly. Crows like to feed in the early morning and then again in the afternoon. Make sure you put food out at those times.

Calling All Crows!

Crows communicate with each other constantly through a variety of calls. You can learn to make some of these crow calls yourself to attract and observe crows in the crow corner of your backyard. While there are electronic calls you can buy at local outdoor stores, you will have more fun making them with your own voice.

Safari Tip
If you have a vegetable garden in your backyard, you'll want to protect it from crows as well as other birds and animals. With an adult's help, build a fence around the garden, or put wire screening around the individual plants.

What Do I Need?

- Your hands and voice
- A bush or tree to hide behind
- A notebook and pen or pencil

What Do I Do?

- Go behind the tree, bush, or some other place where you can't be easily seen.
- Cup your hands in front of your mouth and try the different calls listed on the next page.
- Observe the response of the crows that appear after hearing your call and write it down in your notebook.

Crow Calls to Try:

- Rally Call – A crow will give this call to other crows to bring them together—maybe to eat some newfound food, such as carrion. Repeat: CAAAWWW, CAAAWWW, CAAAWWW.
- Fight Call – This is a call to drive off predators or other intruders in crow territory. It could be a call for mobbing. It is best to do this call with a few other friends or family members that can spread out across your backyard. Make loud growling sounds and mix them with high screeches.
- Danger Call – This call is a warning to other crows that a predator is nearby and that they should flee. It consists of fast, high-pitched short calls of CAW-CAW-CAW.
- Attention-Grabbing Call – A crow makes this sound when it is showing off to other crows. The crow is saying, "look at me." Repeat CAW-AW, CAW-AW quickly.

Don't expect to become an expert crow caller right away. Listen to crow calls on a website, such as Crows.net. Or, better yet, listen to the calls of the crows that visit your backyard. You might want to record the crow calls with a portable tape recorder or a cell phone and then play them back and imitate them. The more you practice, the better you'll become at it. More crows will listen and think that they've found a new friend!

Join The Crows.net Project

Crows.net is a website dedicated to providing information about crows. The site has a project where it collects data about crows and their behavior from "crow fanciers," who are everyday people like you. You can be part of the Crows.net Project by keeping records of your observations of the crows in your backyard.

A scarecrow in a cornfield doesn't scare off these two crows.

What Do I Need?

- A notebook and pen or pencil
- A pair of binoculars
- A computer with Internet access

What Do I Do?

- Record your observations of the crows that visit your backyard. Look particularly for any unusual behavior. One person reported seeing a crow flying with a whole piece of pizza in its beak!
- Use your computer to type your observations and then email them to crows.net@gmail.com. Be sure to include your name, the town or city you live in, your state, and the date or dates of your observations.

❊ If you have any questions about crows, you may submit them as well on a form provided on the website. All submissions will be posted on the website, unless you ask them not to.

Counting Crows

We're not talking about the rock group that goes by that name, but actually counting the number of crows you see in your backyard or crow corner.

The website eBird.org is an online checklist operated by the Cornell Lab of **Ornithology** and the National Audubon Society. To date, it has 30,000 people reporting more than one million bird sightings. The eBird website is free to all birdwatchers. You create a username and password, and then log in and report your observations on the crows or other birds you have seen in your yard at any time of year. Anyone living in North America, Central America, and the Caribbean can take part in this ongoing program. Visit www.ebird.org for more information.

Enjoy your time with these clever, fascinating birds and have a happy safari!

Glossary

captivity the state of being held captive, such as an animal in a cage

carrion the dead flesh of animals

defecate to discharge, or pass, waste from the bowels

grub the wormlike larva of an insect

habitat an area where an animal naturally lives and develops

mobbing an act of many crows or other birds surrounding and annoying another bird or animal until it is driven away

molt the process of a bird shedding feathers that will be replaced by new feathers

omen a sign or warning that signals either good or bad luck

ornithology the scientific study of birds

plumage all the feathers that cover the body of a bird

predator an animal that preys on, or hunts, other animals for food

roost to rest or sleep on a perch such as a tree branch

species one type of animal within a larger category

virus disease-causing microorganisms

Find Out More

Books

Bradley, James V. *Crows and Ravens (Nature Walk).* New York: Chelsea Clubhouse, 2006.

National Geographic Learning. *Crows (Smart Animals).* Independence, KY: National Geographic School Publications, 2010.

Pringle, Laurence. *Crows! Strange and Wonderful.* Honesdale, PA: Boyds Mills Press, 2010.

Websites

A Murder of Crows: Crow Facts

www.pbs.org/wnet/nature/episodes/a-murder-of-crows/introduction/5838

Learn many fascinating facts about crows and watch the entire television episode from PBS's *Nature* series about these birds.

All About Birds: American Crow

www.allaboutbirds.org/guide/american_crow/id

Learn all about how to identify crows, their behavior, and habits, and hear and see them in audio and video clips.

Frequently Asked Questions about Crows

www.birds.cornell.edu/crows/crowfaq.htm

Find lots of fascinating answers to common questions about crows on this website.

Index

Page numbers in **boldface** are illustrations.

About the Author

STEVEN OTFINOSKI has written more than 160 books for young readers, many of them about animals ranging from koalas to scorpions. Growing up, his pets included turtles, cats, and dogs. He lives in Connecticut with his wife, their daughter, and two dogs.